When it comes to money, you can only move

forward or backwards.

Table of Contents

Introduction

Step 1: Financial Health, p. 6

Step 2: Powerful Strategies to Increasing Income, p. 17

Step 3: Dynamic Ways to Squashing Debt Forever, p. 21

Step 4: Vital Steps to Getting Budget on Track, p. 64

Step 5: Effortless Ways to Build Savings & Retirement, p. 80

Step 6: Achieve Life-Changing Wealth, p. 90

Conclusion, p. 94

Introduction

Welcome and thank you for your purchase.

The purpose of this book is to teach you what our school systems and the corporate world have failed to do. I suspect many of you are in a similar situation of tired of being stuck in the failing middle class. It's a true statement that the rich get richer, and the poor get poorer.

My financial background includes being a commercial credit analyst at a large regional bank, an analyst at a multi-billionaire dollar global investment firm and working at the Pentagon helping to budget billions of dollars to help our great service members accomplish their mission and to keep America safe.

Often referred to as "Debt Snowball" or sometimes "Debt Stacking", both terms are synonymous. These strategies are approaches that I learned the hard way. Having graduated high school just before the dot-com crash, I was educated by society and banks that I needed credit cards to build debt. With credit, you cannot make it in this world. With the lure of easy purchasing and simple payment plans, I quickly found myself caught in a web of debt.

With no help in sight, it led me down a painful path that eventually led me to study and understanding finance. Later with my experience and research, I quickly learned that we are slaves to the financial institutions from mortgages to student loan debt. How can anyone achieve financial freedom when they cannot escape the web of lies and debt?

That is why this book is written. Having studied and discussed with billionaires and millionaires, I've learned a few common trends which I am sharing in this book.

The insight and purpose to help the middle class, led me to start my website DollarOtter.com which aims to help families "Achieve Financial Freedom". That is the sole purpose and mission. Join me on this journey as we dive into this material!

Nick | Dollar Otter

To my children, Liam & Rylinn, you can accomplish anything if you put the Lord first and work hard with determination.

STEP 1

Financial Health

Financially Illiterate Society

There is a reason why so many households don't discuss money or budget with friends or family. Also, many families don't purchase finance books because they are led to believe they know everything about money.

In 2017, a financial services company, Financial Engines[1], put this to the test. They conducted a survey with only 11 questions in which only 6% of the respondents passed.

Reflecting back on my education and having completed a Masters in Finance and an MBA in Finance, I never took a class or one hour lecture of household budgeting. I do recall one high school class teaching me how to write a check. Hmmm..how to spend money but not make money or manage my money?

Finances can have a negative connotation too. Think about failed marriages or fighting in the household over money. What is the first thing that usually comes up during family discussions after a loved-one passes on? This divides families because society hasn't managed it properly.

What is Financial Literacy?

Investopedia.com describes financial literacy as "the education and understanding of various financial areas including topics related to managing personal finance, money and investing".[2]

It is almost an epidemic plague. Since 2003, the United States recognizes the month of April as "Financial Literacy Month" and has done so since 2003. During this time, free events are hosted, free materials are distributed to highlight the economic importance of having a basic financial education. Campaigns advised those who attended to use the hashtags to share stories (#MySavingsStory). The Senate hosted a "Financial Literacy Day on Capitol Hill"[3] to show their support behind this crucial illness.

How to Improve Your Literacy

After reading this book, you will have a greater understanding of money than 90% of society. First, you are going to be introduced to some basic stats so you can understand how big of an issue this has become.

In 2017, CareerBuilder conducted a survey which the results plagued the media. Their survey concluded that "78% of U.S. workers live paycheck to paycheck to make ends meet"[4] and approximately 75% are in debt.

I've heard numerous times from clients "If I made more money, I wouldn't have money problems or debt". Working at an investment firm, I knew one of the portfolio managers who retired after making $25 million one year. He retired that year to live out his dream and goal of sailing around the world and living the good life. He returned 3 years later because he spent every dime of his fortune.

The issue isn't how much you make…it's how you manage your money.

"Having a higher salary doesn't necessarily mean money woes are behind you, with nearly one in 10 workers making $100,000 or more (9 percent) saying they usually or always live paycheck-to-paycheck and 59 percent in that income bracket in debt."[4]

Next, you should recognize that a large financial burden is on the horizon. Economists don't know when, yet; but sooner or later the bill will be due. "43% of student loan borrowers are not making payments."[5] How is it that being in this country [United States] with more education than ever, society lacks the basic ability to manage our money or finances?

Banks and the federal government want consumers to borrow. Borrowing makes them money and the government knows borrowing moves the economy. We've seen a 213% increase in tuition at public universities over the past 30 years[5], the average student debt is $32,731 according to the Federal Reserve.[6]

So we need to ask the question...if education is so important, why do we allow the interest rates of financing a home and automobiles to be significantly lower than financing student loans? As a capitalist, I am all for charging some monetary fee or interest rate for borrowing, but this is a serious problem. "According to a report by LendEDU, the average fixed rate on a private student loan is currently just under 10%, while the average interest rate on a variable loan is just under 8%."[7] See any issues with this now?

Third, the average U.S. household struggles to come with $400 for emergency situations; however, many families have been saving with an average of just over $16,000 in savings accounts[8]. So depending on which statistic you refer to, it does paint a picture that many families are hurting while others are doing well.

Experian conducted a study to obtain a snapshot of the average balance on credit cards. In 2017, the average balance was $6,354 and had an average mortgage balance of $201,811.[9] How do you align with these stats?

I share these statistics and numbers in this material so you have an understanding of how money is working around us. Later we dive into saving but you need to understand that debt is an epidemic that is plaguing society.

Understanding Net Worth

Determining your net worth is an important component of knowing where your financial situation is currently. It allows you to see where you are on your journey and how much further you have to go to reach your final destination.

The Federal Reserve reports the average net worth for families for the following age groups:

< 35: $76,200

35-44: $288,700

45-54: $727,500

55-64: $1,167,400

Your net worth is the difference between what you own (assets) from what you owe (liabilities/debt). If you are a business owner, it is the net equity of your business. It provides you with a snapshot of how much you own or owe if you had to liquidate everything.

If you are unsure what your current net worth is, I highly recommend you visit PersonalCapital.com to calculate. The website offers a Free net worth calculation.

The formula for Net Worth is Financial Assets - Financial Liabilities

What to Include in Assets?

Assets to include in this category are cash/money in bank accounts (checking, savings), Certificates of Deposits (CDs), stocks, bonds, investments, mutual funds, jewelry, automobiles, home, etc. Basically, anything you can sell for cash.

If you own a business, you can add these assets to it as well (the portion of what you own if you have a partner).

There are several different types of values to consider when determining your net worth. There is market value, resale value, book value, etc. For the everyday household, I recommend market value. This will describe what the value of an asset is should you be forced to sell today.

For automobiles, obtain the Kelly Blue Book value while Zillow can be a benchmark value if you haven't had your home appraised in quite some time. Research jewelry, computers, and other valuables on eBay and see what the selling price is going for from consumers.

What to Include in Liabilities?

To determine your financial liabilities, you'll need to inquire about the payoff amounts from the lenders. The payoff amount is not always the same as what is reflected in the statements. This is because some debts will have additional interest between the time the statement was mailed to you and the time you inquire about the payoff balance.

Liabilities include loans such as mortgages, a line of equities, retail and credit cards, consumer and personal loans, automobiles, student loans, etc.

To revisit the calculation of Net Worth, you'll need to determine the current values of your assets and liabilities. Then using the chart below, subtract your liabilities from the assets.

Formula: Assets - Liabilities = Net Worth

Net Worth Calculation

ASSETS	LIABILITIES

Total Assets: Total Liabilities:

NET WORTH:

Note: Read my blog on Calculating Net Worth

(https://www.dollarotter.com/blank-2/Why-You-Need-to-Calculate-Your-Net-Worth)

[1] Financial Literacy Quiz. FinancialEngines.com. https://financialengines.com/financial-literacy-quiz

[2] Financial Literacy. Investopedia. https://www.investopedia.com/terms/f/financial-literacy.asp

[3] Financial Literacy Month. Council for Economic Education. https://www.councilforeconed.org/financial-literacy-month/

[4] Press Release. August 24, 2017. CareerBuilder. http://press.careerbuilder.com/2017-08-24-Living-Paycheck-to-Paycheck-is-a-Way-of-Life-for-Majority-of-U-S-Workers-According-to-New-CareerBuilder-Survey

[5] 4 Stats that Reveal How Badly America is Failing at Financial Literacy. 3 April 2018. Forbes. https://www.forbes.com/sites/danipascarella/2018/04/03/4-stats-that-reveal-how-badly-america-is-failing-at-financial-literacy/#616c0de2bb7b

[6] Report on the Economic Well-Being of U.S. Households in 2016-May 2017. Federal Reserve. https://www.federalreserve.gov/publications/2017-economic-well-being-of-us-households-in-2016-education-debt-loans.htm

[7] What's the Average Student Loan Interest Rate? Debt Management. 19 March 2018. SoFi. https://www.sofi.com/resource-center/debt-management/whats-average-student-loan-interest-rate/

[8] How much does the average US household have in a savings account? 26 September 2018. Motley Fool contribution to USA Today. . https://www.usatoday.com/story/money/personalfinance/budget-and-spending/2018/09/26/how-much-average-household-has-savings/37917401/

[9] Sullivan, Bob. 11 January 2018. State of Credit: 2017. Experian. https://www.experian.com/blogs/ask-experian/state-of-credit/

STEP 2

Powerful Strategies to

Increasing Income

Writing

While it is very difficult to make a lot of money from selling ebooks, it is a great way to earn passive income. I have been selling the same ebooks on Amazon for two years now with consistent income anywhere from $5-$25 a month. While it isn't anything substantial, it is regular income that I don't have to keep promoting. I recommend you google KDP Amazon to get started.

Selling

When it comes to business, our minds immediately go to selling something. This "something" is either a good or service and with the advancements in technology today, there is no excuse for anyone not to make money.

People are quick to make excuses about not making enough or the challenges they face. After my divorce, I had liquidated most of my savings and retirement to pay for legal fees. Faced with the option of going into depression or fighting the battle to get back up, I took every advantage to get out of debt and to recover what was lost.

Having launched three online businesses, selling odds and ends, anything possible to make money, I was determined to not allow depression set in. It was during this journey that I discovered income potential.

I sold my online businesses to fund my blog website dollarotter.com and to jump start my retirement savings. To get out of debt, I drove for Lyft every moment I had free time. No excuses!

One terrific way to really earn some great money is eBay. The reason why this is so underutilized is because households don't know what to sell. Here is the secret. Every chance you get, go to neighborhood garage sales and Goodwill stores. Find products that sell really well on eBay. Here is a hint: vintage name brand golf bags and luggage sell well on eBay.

You can usually purchase these items from pennies to a few dollars while selling them for 10 times this at least. I have an antique Kodak camera that I use in my YouTube videos that I purchased for $20. I receive offers up to $200 all the time because something like this is difficult to find. But it wasn't difficult to find for me if you know what to look for.

Offer Services & Products

Entrepreneurs make money by selling products or services. If you have an idea, create a product and sell it online. Maybe you have a skill that you can offer a service.

With so many ideas flooding the marketplace, you need to know that any idea and product can be improved. Technology continues to improve making services and products more affordable, more efficient, and more effective.

Think back to when MySpace was popular. Facebook came along with the same idea only it was redesigned with better features. It was made better.

Amazon offers a service online to sell ebooks to consumers. Are you a good writer? Fiverr allows people to hire people with skills through their online portal. I've done several of these online jobs making thousands. It works and it is effective. Use Google to browse ideas because it is a powerful resource.

STEP 3

Dynamic Ways to Squash

Debt Forever

Analyze Your Spending

When I moved to San Antonio, Texas, I linked up with a brilliant financier. For the sake of privacy, I'll stick with his first name only, David, amazing and talented guy. He showed me the ropes of analyzing why everyday normal families are going broke. It is from him where I discovered 75% of Americans are broke.

Did You Know? 68% of the U.S. economy is made from Consumer Spending.

Statistics gives researchers, marketers, advertisers insight on how consumers are spending their money. The Bureau of Labor Statistics releases an annual Economic News Release reflecting the "average expenditures and income of all consumer units"[1] from food, healthcare, education, cash contributions, and more.

The largest increase in from 2016 to 2017 was education and fuel prices according to that report. Now when talking about analyzing your spending, I am not highlighting economic trends itself, but how you are spending your money and where is the money going.

For instance, how much money did you put into your savings account? What is the current balance of the account? Next, did you max your IRA annual limits?

When I started analyzing my spending, I was shocked by the discovery. I've always found myself of being frugal and rather thrifty. In 2018, I spent $627 on coffee. I highlight this not to brag but to show how trends and data can help us. Knowing that I spend this much on coffee, I can make a cost-conscious decision to cut about 20% of this spending and put to work for me. This equates to $125 in addition to what is already being saved.

The easiest way to determine this is by downloading the app, Clarity Money, to your smartphone. It is a financial app recently purchased by Goldman Sachs as a way to improve their image with Main Street. Regardless of anyone's opinions of the bank, this is a great app to track anything financial. More on it later.

Review Bank Statements

On a regular basis, minimum monthly, you should review your banking statements. If you are budgeting, determine where you have exceeded your budget and why. Determine what your bank statements are saying about you as a spender and a saver. Then ask yourself if you like what you are seeing.

How much did you save last month? Can you save more? If not, why not?

Overspending is the enemy to every budget. Take a highlighter and mark where you spent more money than you should have spent. Now ask yourself, "Am I willing to spend less and will I spend less next month?"

"Overspending is the enemy to every budget."

Review Credit Card Statements

You're thinking to yourself, "Do I have to do this budget exercise?" The answer is yes. Credit card companies are sneaky! When financial institutions discovered Americans were starting to pay off their credit cards and were seeking ways to get out of debt, they created new incentives to push you to keep swiping those plastic cards.

The incentives are being awarded points, dollars, airline miles, etc. Think about it. According to Investopedia, "When merchants accept payments via credit card, they are required to pay a percentage of the transaction amount as a fee to the credit card company...The goal is to incentivize people to use their credit cards when making payments rather than cash or debit cards"[2].

Credit cards making spending money too easy. This is why three-fourths of the U.S. economy is in debt. "Credit is most perilous when you make consumption purchases you can't afford in the first place"[3]. It is difficult to pay off credit cards if you keep using the cards.

When reviewing your credit card spending habits, are you paying your balance in full every month to eliminate any credit charges?

Your challenge is to stop using your credit cards and start paying with cash.

Is Credit Bad?

Can you imagine a lifestyle of not having easy credit readily available to you? When cash flow is short and emergencies arise, credit cards come very handily for such situations. Credit can be helpful, useful, and dangerous--all in one if you are not careful.

The first type of credit acquired by consumers are those plastic cards we swipe and later owe the financial institution money. Credit cards are short-term solutions with potential long-term effects. Such effects include overly high monthly principal payments and monthly debt payments, mid-to-high interest rates, and reversing your income building potential.

What the Credit Card Companies Don't Want You To Know

This type of debt carries what is known in the financial industry as Revolving Debt. According to LendingTree.com, "revolving debt consists of open-ended accounts, usually with variable interest rates, predetermined credit limits, and payments that are calculated as a percentage of the unpaid balance".

Unlike a regular automobile loan or most mortgages where the interest is usually fixed and the monthly payments remain the same, credit cards can fluctuate its rates. One month your rate may be 12% but the following month it may be 12% + market rate (3.25%).

This is one reason why credit cards can be dangerous.

The other reason is the minimum payment due. As rates increase, so may the monthly minimum amount each month. One month your minimum payment could reflect $200 while the next month you may $400!

When you are budgeting your finances, it can be very difficult to forecast this payment. If you under forecast, it will offset another item from within your budget. This is why I highly encourage my readers to get mentally strong and recognize that your debt should be paid off as fast as possible.

You may be thinking to yourself now..."I received a 0% interest for 12 months in the mail. Do I take the offer?" I think it is something to consider if you understand that opening a new credit account will lower your credit score potentially by a few points in the first few months. Also, you must be disciplined enough not to use the available credit from the card you transferred the balance over to the new card.

A very common mistake that households make when receiving such offers is once a credit balance with a high-interest rate is transferred to a zero percent introductory rate card, they "perceive" available credit as an opportunity to spend more on the old card. Don't do this! It defeats the point of the transfer and now instead of having one monthly payment, you will have two payments.

This is why credit cards can be dangerous.

Other types of credit may be used to purchase a home or an automobile. It is highly encouraged that if you are mortgaging a home, then strive for a 15-year fixed mortgage. Most household budgets can't afford this so they turn towards a 30-year mortgage and almost always accept the point that they will pay twice as much for the house in that time frame.

When it comes to auto loans, it is always best to avoid getting an auto loan but Simple Dollar has a resource available "Best Auto Loans for 2018" to help get you started so if you need to borrow, you can do it responsibly.

It all boils down to your self-discipline. Continuous spending increases your lifestyle. The trick is to find a balance and maintain your lifestyle for as long as possible.

The theory is as more income comes your way, you are saving it for the future. When you try to keep up with the Joneses, you outspend, overspend, and get into financial trouble. Recognize that it is okay not to have everything and start to condition your mind differently to live more simple.

Debt Snowball

Often referred to as "Debt Snowball" or sometimes "Debt Stacking", both terms are synonymous. These strategies are approaches in paying off debt in the most meaningful and efficient manner possible. It consists of both mathematical and psychological formulas that may sound difficult but in practice is very easy and simple.

Let me first state that I understand what it is like being in debt. At 18, I quickly fumbled into credit card debt without a full-time job because I wasn't taught the basic principles of managing money. Nor did I understand the impacts of interest payments and its devastation it can cause.

On this page, I want to share with you an approach that financial institutions apply because it is effective and saves money in interest payments.

Step 1 Devise a Plan: Sort and organize your debt by highest interest rate to lowest. Next determine which bill has the lowest balance that can be paid in 2-4 months. After creating your priority list, it is time to devise a plan to be debt free.

Write down the monthly payment amount due from each bill. The payment plan should help you to pay off the priority loans easily so you will be making minimum payments on the bills ranked from #2 and on. This focuses the payments on bill #1 to quickly pay that off so in the next month once paid off, that payment can be applied to debt #2.

So try to put all the extra money towards the payment of the loans. You can also make double payments to decrease the repayment amount. In case of the other smaller loans, you can make the minimum payments until you are ready to pay them off.

Step 2 Establish Automatic Payments: To be debt free quickly, use the automatic repayment method. The best option to make timely repayment is to set up an automatic repayment from your bank account. This can save you a lot of time and also be assured that the payments will be made on time. There is no need to fear about deferring the payments. However, ensure that your account has the amount during that time. By following these procedures, you can easily clear all your debt to be debt free.

Additional Minimum Payment Plan

Imagine filling up a pool with a garden hose only this garden hose is pouring out just enough water as what is evaporating from the pool. No matter how long you fill up the pool, the water level never seems to change.

The minimum payment on credit cards is very similar to this concept. No matter how long you pay on the credit card, if you are not paying more than the minimum monthly requirement, you will never pay off that debt. You must pay more than what the minimum amount is to reduce it. Apparently, the more you can pay on your balance, the quicker you can pay it off.

Balance Transfer

There are moments when I recommend you transfer your credit card balance to a zero-percent interest rate card, whether as an introductory period of a new card or an existing card.

Many consumers may make the mistake of canceling their cards after the transfer, but this action has a negative consequence on your credit score. It is better to have the paid off card remain active but DO NOT use the card again. Instead allow the card to remain active and receive the benefit of it improving your credit score as your credit utilization percentage, which is ranked by credit agencies, to work towards your advantage.

Personal Loan Game

One of the most rewarding aspects about this website is being able to help my friends and family get their financial affairs in order.

To be honest, I had hesitation at first putting this website up because while I have a talent for key aspects in this industry, I never enjoy giving financial advice that has risk potential. Mostly out of fear that "what if I am wrong this time?".

It is my own fear that I deal with but the more I ponder on it, the more it shows proof of my caring for them and their finances and my due diligence is valuable to them.

Money is a private and sensitive topic for anyone to discuss; yet, the majority of the population are seeking help and want such valuable advice!

It is good for you to discuss finances with those close to you. I always encourage men to discuss their finances with their spouses! We are guilty at times, especially if we handle the budgeting, to keep our finances secret. Usually it is because we don't like to fail and when budgets go into the red, it proves we are no longer Superman.

Now that we are warmed up, let's briefly discuss whether one should get a loan to payoff credit cards. Many of you know but some readers out there checking this website this website for the first time may not know, that credit cards charge a Revolving Rate. This means a rate is consistently calculated...DAILY!

How on earth can anyone pay a credit card charging 18% or more APR? These types of loans are not fixed liked an automobile where rates are usually from 4-6% annually. At least with fixed rate loans the interest payment steadily declines as the principal payment increases.

If it weren't for revolving debt, financial firms wouldn't make their money-well large sums of money. Oddly enough, when you walk into your bank [true story], a banker is asked if one should pay off a credit card or get a consumer loan to pay it off.

The banker who has a conflict of interest obviously will usually say something along the lines of "One should continue to payoff the credit card making more than minimum payment." I've even heard some say, paying it off will harm your credit score. Get a free copy of your credit score with a company I trust, Credit

Sesame.

If you are disciplined enough to NOT USE your credit card and you have a substantial balance that is difficult to payoff, then I do recommend you get a consumer loan to pay off the debt.

Why you ask?

Well, it boils down to interest payments. If you have Credit Card "A" that is charging you 18% APR compared to Consumer Loan "B" with a fixed interest rate of 6%, which loan do you think you can pay off first? Most likely the 6% rate loan assuming the borrowed amount was roughly the same amount.

Also, with Consumer Loan "B" the payments are fixed unlike credit cards which help you manage a better forecasted budget. But I must stress the importance of NOT USING your credit cards while these loan payments are being made.

If you happen to be thinking about such options with a banker, then here are some things that do decide your credit score in this video below.

Sometimes particular situations warrant you the chance to payoff your credit card with a loan. In cases like these, I personally use SoFi. Yes, I have used this company in the past because of the staff's professionalism and courtesy. Most importantly, the turn around time to process and receive the deposit was the same day. This isn't to say, you will get the same day turn around.

If you happen to have a credit score with some bruises on it, then take a few minutes to discuss this with the Credit Assistance Network. They are rated A+ by the Better Business Bureau and can provide a FREE CREDIT ANALYSIS.

Another great resource to use is Lending Tree. You can shop rates from the convenience of your home or office.

BEFORE YOU TAKE OUT A LOAN, I WANT TO ENCOURAGE YOU TO TAKE MY ONLINE COURSE "4 WAYS TO PAYOFF DEBT".

This course is designed to walk you through a process known as Debt Stacking. Some refer to it as Debt Snowball. This course sells for $19.99 but if you use promo code

DOLLAROTTER10 you can take it for $9.99 or less depending on the specials running by Udemy.com.

Remember when it comes to debt, be sure you are discussing strategies and talking to your spouse or significant other about it so you can get on the same page and start tackling this amount down quickly.

Money moves in three ways, Up, Down or Sideways. Be sure you are taking the steps to move your money Up.

Cutting Expenses

As the holiday season is officially upon us, nothing screams "Help!" like your wallet. Below I've listed 10 ways to help you save money this year by making some minor adjustments to your daily routine or spending habits.

#1 Cutting Cable

Did you know the average subscriber spends $85 per month on cable services? A recent study conducted by Leichtman Research reflects households are cutting the cord on cable. In fact, approximately 754,000 subscribers cut their cable during the second quarter of 2018. As a result of this, cable companies saw an increase of 383,000 subscribers moving to stream services, particularly in DirecTV Now and Sling TV.

I wish I could say this shocked me but after looking for ways to cut my budget expenses down, I canceled my DirecTV service and started a DirecTV Now subscription. This saved me 66% on my cable expense as my bill went from $120 to $40 plus with the special offer over the summer, I received a Free Apple TV as well as no bill until Oct 1. For me, this was a Win-Win!

This is why cutting your cable bill is ranked #1 on the list because you do not have to rid your cable altogether but rather look for ways to reduce the bill. If you happen to be addicted to the cable service you have and are still in doubts about canceling it, then there are a few other ways to cut costs.

Take a look at your latest bill and review the fees listed. You may see additional programs listed for channels you aren't watching. I noticed that I was paying an additional $10 per month for HBO but hadn't watched anything on that channel in two months. This was a great cost-cutting measure. Another strategy that many consumers never act on is calling your cable company and negotiate your cable bill. Before I got DirecTV Now, I use to do this every 6 months because companies want to keep their base customers. My $120 bill would get slashed to half.

#2 Reduce Your Power Usage

When it comes to saving money, it is the little daily actions taken that stack up to big monthly savings. One of the little daily changes is watching your electrical use. This is one of the bills where you have control and decide how much to consume. While I am not saying to turn off your breaker and live in the dark, I am saying take small actions. Here are several ways in how to reduce your electricity bill.

The first strategy is obvious. Turn off the lights when not using them. This is a difficult habit for many but making this a regular habit and kindly reminding other family members, just saving $1 a day quickly adds up to $30 in savings. Also, check for appliances that are plugged in and not being used. Unplugging regular appliances in the kitchen and bathroom can save you some change.

Another strategy is to minimize the use of your microwave. By thawing frozen foods in your refrigerator before cooking or rather than defrosting in your microwave has substantial savings since these amazing appliances use so much energy.

While there are multiple other strategies, my favorite is replacing your light bulbs with energy efficient LED. I have to be honest. I was not on board with this at first but after taking the challenge, I replaced all my bulbs with the CREE LED bulbs and I saw a $40 savings on my next electricity bill. My home was surrounded with floodlighting and landscape lights. After replacing these with low watt LEDs, it made a huge saving impact while keeping the golden glow that I love on my exterior home.

#3 Reduce Your Grocery Bill

Are you thinking I'm going to write about coupons? I do recommend to use when applicable but rather you will learn some household tricks to having a lower food bill.

The first trick is to stop buying bagged lettuce/mixed greens. This came as a total shocker for me because it's fast, simple, and affordable, or so I thought. Bagged lettuce spoils quickly and when you compare the cost of it to that of a head of romaine lettuce, the head will last longer and you are likely to replace it as often—hence saving money. Plus it is fresher.

Secondly, if you buy potatoes, are you having to replace these weekly because of the root growth? I do until I read an article on preserving these root plants. Once you arrive home with your newly purchased potatoes, place these in a paper bag and store in a dark cool place (not the refrigerator). The paper will allow the water vapors to escape easily thereby saving your potato from rot or root growth. I've been told you can keep these up to about a month and with winter approaching, it's a great way to save some money.

Thirdly, cut back on frozen prepared meals. This can be difficult if you are a busy bee and rarely have time to cook. The truth is frozen meals are costly when compared to making this yourself. You can buy spaghetti, sauce, and make your meatballs that will produce about 4-6 meals for under 5 dollars. This is practically $1 per meal compared to eating out which usually ranges from

$7-$12. Huge savings! Another trick is learning to cook meals in a crockpot. You can easily prep these meals in less than an hour and have the crock pot cook all day. Once cooked, you freeze it to have additional frozen meals.

#4 Stop Paying for Monthly Subscriptions

Have you totaled your monthly subscription service bills from companies like Netflix, Amazon Prime, clothing box services, or personal hygiene box subscriptions? If not, you should consider this because you may be surprised that you're spending over $100 per month. It is easy to be enticed in these low-cost monthly subscriptions from $9.99 to $14.99 or more but if you have too many, this can be detrimental to your finances.

I love the marketing and health benefits of a certain weekly food box delivery. The issue with such services is the total cost per meal. You will easily pay from $10 to $13 a plate. When you have a family, it is very expensive to feed those mouths weekly. This is why I switched to $5 Meal Plans. I have cut my food budget drastically with easy to prep meals and it allows me to cook extra meals for the work week. The savings from cutting back on monthly services have saved me over $100 per month because when I am honest with myself, I don't need these. I just want them.

#5 Pay Off Credit Cards

The average interest rate in the U.S., as of 2018, is 13.08%. Consumers are accustomed to paying high interest rates on credit cards while others use their cards charging zero interest. If you are one of the lucky ones paying no interest, then this tip isn't for you. If you are paying interest then take a look at your credit card statement and total the sum of interest you have paid since January.

Odds are, you could have paid off the card already using the interest you paid the bank. So pay off those credit cards so can you start putting some cash back into your pocket.

#6 Bring Lunch to Work

If you paid $6 per lunch, five days a week, that sums up to $30 per week or $120 per month. This is a very low figure too because lunches usually cost from $8-$12.

It can be tempting to want to socialize with your colleagues if they are going out to eat during lunch. While I don't want you to be anti-social, you must limit such occasions to once per week.

By meal prepping, you can save a lot of money from dining out. People tend to eat healthier too when they bring their lunch and a great way to prep is with PlateJoy. I've been using this company to plan my meals since April and the meals are delicious. They make it easy to shop for key items and most meals can be prepped in 10-15 minutes.

#7 Limit Your App Purchases

Similar to Spring cleaning, I recommend you perform a Fall cleaning within your smartphone. Going through the active purchases, determine how much you can save by cancelling all the apps. Next, determine which apps are a must keep and which ones are not necessities.

This is a win-win situation because not only are you saving money, but you'll free up some space on your phone and it may even perform better.

#8 Overpaying for Insurance

Currently I am licensed to sell Life Insurance in Texas and more often than I not, I see more and more people being overcharged. This upsets me because I see families being taken advantage of everyday but by salesmen who care about nothing but their pockets. The difficult part is determining if you are overpaying.

My tip to families is to always shop around to get "comparable" quotes. Browse several companies and ensure the coverage is the same throughout. Always buy term, never whole life and ensure you get enough coverage to pay off all the bills, put your kids through college, and allow your spouse retire. This is the standard benchmark to aim for because in the worst possible situation, that's how you need to plan.

Another tip is to look to see if you are overpaying for auto insurance too. Consumers have a tendency to stick with one company with one quote forever and while companies are always lowering and raising rates, consumers never call to get a check up on a lower quote.

To get you started, here are a few resources to help you shop. Receive a quote from USAA Life Insurance, eSurance for auto and home, and Navy Mutual for life insurance.

#9 Avoid Overdraft Fees

These fees are outrageous. If you bounce a check, the bank and the company will both charge anywhere from $25-$50 each. This means you are charged $50-$100 for money you already don't have. With proper budgeting, you can eliminate this unnecessary hassle. One of my favorite banks is USAA because they charge absolutely $0 to bank, I get reimbursed my ATM fees if I use a competitor's ATM, and the customer service is superior!

#10 Buy Used

This is self explanatory. This can be applied to everything from cars to clothes. Yes, clothes too! With a company like THREDUP, the company buys your used clothes and then sells the secondhand items to buyers online. Used items are less expensive as some life has been exhausted from the item but you also can receive significant discounts from retail price.

When it comes to saving money, take a look at your purchases. By examining your bank account and credit card statements, the evidence is uncovered on your spending habits. Anyone can save money and by taking just a few small adjustments in your daily habits, you can stack up the savings.

Credit Reports

It all happened in a miraculous moment...a moment like no other. After being outbid over and over due to a hot housing market, the perfect home was sought after.

It was destiny. Now I am at the mercy of the bank...where now I must play by their rules.

The mortgage banker walked over with a strong poker face and me with my thoughts running around a million miles per hour of calculating every point in the interest is more money out of my pocket and what did my credit score state about me.

Knowing my credit is solid, I was more curious about the interest rate. When she quoted this mortgage interest rate, I was pleasantly surprised. I was prepared and had already obtained a free credit report.

My research and keen attention to detail in keeping my bills in line and understanding my credit score worked in my favor this time.

I am flesh and blood and I always learn from my mistakes. You see my credit score used to be something I was very embarrassed about.

I was ashamed because I didn't understand finance and my first credit card was given to me at 18 (a very dangerous game). I quickly racked up $2,500 in debt while finishing high school and then going to college.

My minimum wage job of $4.25/hour wasn't enough to keep the pace of the interest rate being punished upon me. This mistake is also what led me to study finance in college. It is then where I discovered the importance of money and its impact.

Knowing what I know now, protecting your credit is vital. With online hackers and other people in our world who lack integrity, are always out to do us financial harm.

I am a fan of Credit Sesame because you can monitor your credit score for free every month. This company is awesome because you will receive daily monitoring alerts in the event something changes on your credit report. It is like having a personal financier consistently monitoring your credit live. Prior to discovering this company, I was paying from $12-$18 a month to have such service from other companies.

If that wasn't enough, Credit Sesame will also provide you with $50,000 in ID theft insurance protection and Fraud Resolution Assistance. Yes for FREE!

In 2012 the Federal Trade Commission (FTC) issued a study per Congressional mandate requiring the FTC to examine consumer errors within the three main credit reporting agencies. In 2015 a follow-up study was performed and as to many surprised consumers, nearly 20% of these consumers had identified errors.[4]

It highlights the importance to regularly review and check for accuracy. Another factor to consider as another reason to verify its accuracy is Identity Theft. I've written an article found in DollarOtter.com, A Victim of Identity Theft stating according to BigCommerce, "96% of Americans with internet access have made an online purchase at some point in their lives, and four in five (80%) have done so in the last month alone.[5]

It used to be that such companies offered their products solely on their website; however, with the clear majority of online shoppers hitting up Social Media, retailers are flocking to social sites to advertise their brands. While simplicity may be convenient, out in the shadows of the tech world lurches a hungry thief waiting for an unsecured network to quickly hack a shopper's credit card information.

In 2016, Bankrate.com reported that 41 million U.S. adults were such victims.[6] Due to this alarming number making up approximately 13% of the U.S. population, the Federal Trade Commission established a site, IdentityTheft.gov.

Don't be a victim of Identity Theft. Protect your sensitive personal information and check it for any irregularities, errors, and check for accuracy.

Report missing or dispute accounts

Should you find any errors or items needing to be corrected, you must contact the company or institution first to address the matter.

If contacted by mail, then ensure you send via certified mail with return receipt. If the matter has been corrected but still reflecting negatively on your credit report, then contact the credit reporting agencies.

Be sure to keep and maintain copies of any disputes and records of such frivolous activity.

According to the FTC, both the company and person are responsible for correcting the information. Follow the steps outlined in the link to further take action:

https://www.consumer.ftc.gov/articles/0151-disputing-errors-credit-reports

8 Steps to Increasing Your Credit Score:

1. Understanding What Determines Your Credit Score

Is your credit score higher or lower than you expect? The goal for anyone is achieving a high credit score. A higher score means lower interest rates if any at all.

It also helps you in getting new debt making the process so much easier.

This is a difficult task for many. It is extremely difficult if you don't know what components make up your credit score.

If you have a credit score of 655, for example, then according to the pie chart above, 65% of your score is determined by:

a. Payment History

b. Credit Utilization

Focusing on these two measures alone will assist in raising your credit score.

The other measures are just as equally important, but let the numbers do the work for you. It is a strategy because 'Time is Money'.

Other factors assisting to determine your score are:

Credit Age - the longer your credit history, the better

Types of Credit - diversify (mortgage, consumer, credit card)

Number of Inquiries - newer credit applications/inquiries hurt your score

2. Review and Dispute Errors

Protect your personal information. It is sensitive and it is YOURS! Check your credit report on a regular basis. Check for any irregularities, errors, and check it for accuracy.

Should you find any errors or items needing to be corrected, you should definitely contact the company with the dispute and address it directly. You can do this by phone or letter.

If contacted by mail, then ensure you send it via certified mail with return receipt.

If the matter has been corrected but still reflect negatively on your credit report, then contact the credit reporting agencies. Make sure you follow that order of sequence.

Be sure to keep and maintain copies of any disputes and records of such frivolous activity.

According to the FTC, both the company and person are responsible for correcting the information. Follow the steps outlined in the link below to further take action:

https://www.consumer.ftc.gov/articles/0151-disputing-errors-credit-reports

3. Make Timely Payments

Paying your debt on time and paying off debt increases your Credit Utilization; one of the most common and best ways for any consumer to raise his or her credit score is by paying down debt.

In terms of credit cards, the utilization rate is how often and how much money is being used. Basically, it is are you charging up your available credit.

When your credit card is charged (you make a purchase), on an item for $500 with a credit limit of $1,000, that utilization has increased from 0% to 50%. The higher the number, the riskier one may be.

Lower utilization is better for credit scores!

This ratio makes up 30 percent of your score, regardless of whether you plan to pay this off or not.

So be sure to make those payments on time and once those payments are made, avoid using your credit cards. Your goal should be seeing those credit balances consistently going down.

4. Avoid Late Payments

When it comes to paying bills, the traditional manner used to be breaking out the checkbook, calculator, and bank statements. Then adding and subtracting from debits and credits to tally up a total to decide how to pay your bills.

The debtor would either go to the bank for payment or write a check and then mail it out to the company requesting payment. These payments could take anywhere from 2-14 days to process.

Today with the vast upgrade in technology, anyone can make a payment in seconds and with this technology, how is it that consumers are still bouncing checks?

Overdraft fees collected by banks in 2016 totaled over $30 billion--not thousands, not millions, but BILLIONS! That's insane and just reflects how people are not managing their money appropriately.

When selecting to use autopay for bills, you can start making online payments to avoid missing a payment. A missed payment could be reflected on your credit score depending when the next payment is made.

When making auto payments, you avoid receiving late charges that companies love to tack on. These fees, similar to overdraft charges, can range from $20-$50 in some cases. Also at risk, is your interest rate. Some companies will increase your rates for missed payments.

Autopay can save you time. With everyone shouting they have no time, now they have no excuse. It's faster in so many aspects from check writing, calculating, driving to the bank or to the post office, etc. Pay it online and you're done.

5. Do Not Close Accounts

You must avoid closing accounts, if possible. I am not referring to paying off loans but rather calling credit card companies to request closing an account while still owing a balance.

Closing credit accounts will not disappear on your credit report but rather reflect "CLOSED" or something along this verbiage.

I bring this up because if you have credit card balances that are past due, credit card companies have the option to close the account without your approval. This will lower your score and you must still pay the balance.

It takes away your credit utilization which is needed!

For many companies, once the account is closed and still reflects a balance, these accounts cannot be reopened.

6. Avoid Opening New Accounts

With the rapid pace of consumer advertising and marketing for credit, you are offered low rates on credit cards, mortgages, and auto loans every time you turn on the TV, check email or driving on a highway only to see billboards.

It's so frequent and accessible, it's easy to forget the potential impacts of your credit rating. Of course, it always feels rewarding to be approved.

It is not uncommon to see consumers' credit FICO score drop temporarily when one has been approved for new credit. If you paid attention to the pie chart above, you remember "inquiries".

Having recent inquiries up to two years on your credit report may potentially drop your credit score. Therefore, avoid opening too many lines of credit or applying for new cards and applications.

7. Diversify Your Credit

FICO determines your score based on a blended mix of debt. It looks for accounts you have from credit cards, retail accounts, installment loans, financial services accounts, and mortgage loans.

While you may not need each one, having a blended mix and reflecting responsible on-time payments are crucial and the key to having a better credit score.

When I was establishing my credit score after my 18th birthday, I could never get my score any higher than 702. I struggled with getting a higher score for many years.

As I began to understand credit mix, I realized that a mortgage balance was missing. Several years later, I bought a lovely home and within the following month, my score jumped to 780.

Now I am not recommending you rush out to get a mortgage. It reflects your experience with revolving and installment debt-- diversification.

If you have only one credit card, FICO will determine your lack of diversification.

I am not recommending you go out get loans and more credit cards to diversify your portfolio but this is for your education on the impacts of credit and your credit score.

8. Seek 0% APR Balance Transfers

Typically in the fall season, you will start to see more credit card marketing and advertisements offering 0% interest. This usually occurs as we approach the start of the new year.

This begs to question, "Should I transfer my balance?". It's a great question because transferring balances can save you money in interest payments alone.

If you are working towards paying off a credit card, then it is something to definitely explore. You will want to ensure that no additional fees or balance transfers are included in this introductory offer. These are sometimes considered "Hidden Fees".

Some credit cards carry extremely high interest rates. If you own a card and carry such a burden, then it is ideal to explore this avenue.

Even if the hidden fees are nominal, you may still come out ahead by moving the balance to the 0% credit card as long as the interest rate on the newer card is lower once that introductory period is over.

Everyone's situation is uniquely different. You will want to review your current credit and debt situation regularly. Understanding what impacts your credit score, is the first step in learning how to increase it.

Once you understand the factors and the roles that determine your score, you must make time to review your credit report and dispute any errors. If you have no errors, ensure you are making timely payments and not making any late payments.

You can receive a FREE credit report copy at Credit Sesame to perform your due diligence in making sure you have no errors or disputes.

---

[1] Consumer Expenditures--2017. Economic News Release. 11 September 2018. Bureau of Labor Statistics. https://www.bls.gov/news.release/cesan.nr0.htm

[2] Hayes, Adam. How is Cashback Profitable for Credit Card Companies? 23 October 2018. Investopedia. https://www.investopedia.com/articles/personal-finance/040715/how-cashback-profitable-credit-card-companies.asp

[3] Tyson, Eric. Spending Habits. Personal Finance. p 51. John Wiley & Sons.

[4] FTC Issues Follow-Up Study on Credit Report Accuracy. Federal Trade Commission. 21 January 2015. Retrieved from https://www.ftc.gov/news-events/press-releases/2015/01/ftc-issues-follow-study-credit-report-accuracy

[5] Wallace, Tracey. The Complete Omni-Channel Retail Report: What Brands Need to Know About Modern Consumer Shopping Habits in 2018. BigCommerce. Retrieved from https://www.bigcommerce.com/blog/omni-channel-retail/

[6] Dickler, Jessica. 41 Million Americans have had their identities stolen. CNBC.com. 11 Oct 2016. https://www.cnbc.com/2016/10/10/41-million-americans-have-had-their-identities-stolen.html

STEP 4

Vital Steps to Getting

Budget on Track

Did you know that only "60% of Americans admit they do not budget"[1]? While the number of people who participated in this survey are unknown and I do not know what environment this survey was taken, the percentage doesn't surprise me.

You see, I worked part-time as a financial planner with Primerica and one of my responsibilities was helping families get a budget together. It surprised me at first when every family member I asked "How much do you pay towards your credit cards every month?" during our initial sit down and they do not know. Not having a budget is like taking a road trip without a gas gauge in your car.

This chapter will highlight the importance of budgeting to include providing tips and strategies for faster budgeting to save you time.

Accurately Tracking Expenses

Earlier I referenced the gas gauge which tells the driver how much fuel is in the tank. With the driver knowing how much fuel she has in the gas tank, she is able to make wise and knowledgeable decisions. These decisions include:

Can she make it to work or her son's soccer practice without having to stop for fuel? Will she be able to show her client the house he is interested in which is on the other side of the town? Will she make it to the dinner date?

You get the picture. Budgeting is similar but something something in 1950 that provided extra fuel or reserve tank for the car allowing Susan to drive longer than what is in the fuel tank. Only this fuel was a borrowed 5-gallon jug in her trunk and must be replaced with the 5-gallons but an additional gallon. I am referring to credit cards.

American Express and Diners' Club introduced this form of credit in 1950. Ever since then, the world has been hooked with "easy" money.

When you spend more money than what your paycheck allowed, you are dipping into one of two categories: savings or credit. I believe it is why the average household stopped budgeting. Families are "winging it" until next pay day.

Tracking your expenses is vital if you hope to achieve financial freedom. While you don't have to memorize every single penny in the budget, you MUST have a place to reference your spending. It is your gameplan to reach financial freedom.

The best way to track expenses are pen and paper in my opinion. It is why I offer free budget templates on www.dollarotter.com. I have tried apps, spreadsheets, word documents, but paper is my favorite method because I can quickly reference it. Other families prefer to budget on apps.

Irregardless, it doesn't matter the method but the practice does matter! Get into a habit and record every penny spent.

To track expenses accurately, you have to go to the source of where your money is stored. Usually it is your bank account. Review your bank statements, credit card statements, any receipts saved. You need to analyze and categorize your expenses. Once you purchase something at the store, make a note of it, place the receipt on your budget template, or whatever you need to do so you can accurately record when you have 30 seconds.

Forecasting Expenses

Unlike investing when compliance officers make analysts and portfolio managers note on their investment performance "historical performance is not an indicator of future performance", human behavior is a tremendous way to forecast. Your spending habits over the last few months will most likely tell a story. Did you overspend? Did you save enough? Does your family go to restaurants more than forecasted?

By looking at historical bank statements from the last few months, you can dictate your common spending behavior. I highly recommend you review as far back as 12 months at least once. You'd be surprise how many one-time charges come up throughout the year. Think about annual subscriptions, memberships, auto tag renewal, birthdays, anniversaries, etc.

No budget is going to be perfect every single month but you can hedge your risk but forecasting expenses and then sticking to your budget.

Avoid Spending Splurges

If you have made the conscious decision buckle down on your budget, you will have motivation for several days. Every once in a while, temptation will creep its head around the corner telling you to buy that item on sale in the aisle because it is 50% off. Oh what a deal!

One trick I do is to remind myself what the end goal is. I do this because if I think short-term and look at my bank account, I'm thinking "Well, $20 won't break me." but if I am thinking "No, because that delays my goal by a few days to reaching my $450,000 savings goal." Which is more important to you?

Some helpful tips from MoneySavingExpert.com says to "Sleep on it, work out, focus on your debt/savings" etc.[2]

It is often times during these splurges, spending sprees, overspending moments that tends to get you caught into trouble. You have to condition your mindset to staying focused on your end goal. By avoiding overspending, you are helping your budget stay on track.

Conduct Adequate Research

Most financial planners do not highlight this tip so I am going to share it with you because it has helped me save money over the years. To some families, this comes very natural. Shop around!

I like to price comparison shop. With the advantages of using the internet, it is so easy now. Even stores like Amazon will match or beat competitors' pricing if you show the store's manager. While society considers this cheap, I consider it a step of saving a few Benjamin's which helps me reach my goal faster. Who doesn't like a sale?

Conduct your research adequately for prices and don't beat yourself up if you cannot find a better price. Sometimes this happens but it is a great resource that puts a big smile on your budget's face.

Boosting Income

A common plague that wipes out most household budgets is the lack of income. This is usually a result of not saving enough money and living off of debt (credit cards). It is why I am such a huge advocate for working another job.

After my divorce, I was faced with over $89,000 (non-mortgage) debt. This was a combination of credit cards, personal loans, etc. With an income of $80,000 plus paying child support etc, I had this plague visit my budget.

It is what led me down the adventure of sucking up my pride and finding creative new ways to make money. I knew in my heart that if I worked smartly, I could make extra income to pay off the debt. I didn't care if I worked 18 hour days. My focus was so sharp and clear because I had an end result in mind. It was to be debt-free.

I have written several blogs on ways to make extra income. Go to dollarotter.com/blog and you will find several articles. It also helped me to land a part-time job working at Primerica. It is there where I learned that outside of investing, I could earn passive income.

Earning passive income is one of the greatest income tools you can achieve. It is not easy and takes a lot of work. The greatest thing about passive income once established, is it continues to pay you--even when you are not working.

Paying Cash

Most people don't consider paying cash for anything today. It has almost become synonymous with paying with a debit card. I write paying with cash because something households have a habit of overspending. If you are one of these families that continue to overcharge, overspend, etc, consider putting yourself on a cash only program.

It is very difficult to overcharge anything if you are paying cash for stuff.

When I had difficulties staying in my budget percentage for grocery shopping, I would drive to an ATM and withdraw the cash amount in my grocery category. I would never use my debit card and would purposely leave it at home. This forced me to shop smartly and carefully. I remember putting items back onto the shelves because it busted my dollar limit. It is humbling and challenging but allowed me to think and spend more wisely.

Avoiding Debt

When Solomon wrote in Proverbs 22:7, "...the borrower is slave to the lender." (NIV), he was truly a wise man and this wisdom is something we need to hold dear to our heart.

Having debt obviously means we owe something of value to someone who lent it to us. Unfortunately, it is all too common in today's world to accept the fact that we collectively owe on average $15,983 in credit card debt, according to NerdWallet as of December 2017.

With all debt to include mortgages, auto loans, and student debt, that number quickly climbs to over $133,568.

The reason why you need to focus on credit card debt first is that of something called "Revolving Debt". Unlike your automobile loan or most mortgages which are a fixed rate (agreed upon rate where interest steadily declines over the course of the payment), revolving debt continually accrues until the debt is gone.

Even if you owe $25 on a revolving debt, you will still be paying interest on it. This is why debt such as credit cards are so financially dangerous unless of course, you are on the lending side in which you are steadily receiving these interest payments.

Because you need to focus on getting rid of this debt, here are my six strategies to guide you towards reaching financial freedom.

Avoid Minimum Payments

Other than the obvious reason that paying the minimum monthly payment keeps you in debt longer, you are willingly paying the credit card companies more money. This money is called interest payments. With a high-interest rate, it can lead you to serious financial trouble and your credit score could potentially take a hit as well.

Think of it this way...you pay the minimum amount because you are basically saying "This is all I can give you right now, but maybe next month I will pay more." Perhaps not exactly, but you are delaying paying off this debt.

According to Ed Mierzwinksi, U.S. Public Interest Research Group, "If you pay twice the amount of the minimum, that repayment period gets cut in half." Regardless of how fast this debt gets paid off, the point is paying the minimum amounts only keeps you in debt longer so avoid this at all possible.

Refuse to Use

When you use your credit card, you are increasing your credit utilization (CU). For instance, if you have zero debt on a card, then your CU is 0. The higher this number moves up, the lower your credit score moves. It has an inverse relationship.

I wrote an ebook on CU and my research has found that this makes up approximately 30% of your credit score. This is quite a large portion of your credit score calculation. If you are interested in learning more, check out my $1 ebook on Amazon, Increase Credit Score in 1 Month.

Negotiate a Lower Interest Rate

Companies want your business. BOTTOM LINE. If you present offers from other credit card companies that are offering lower rates, you stand a good chance that your company will lower the rate a few basis points in order to keep your business. Sometimes, they refuse but you need to be confident and have a good standing record with this company.

Be sure you have researched and have the offers readily available, know the interest rates you are being offered and currently being charged, know your credit score, and ask to speak to the supervisor when you feel the conversation is getting anywhere with the financial representative. Be polite though!

Apply Debt Snowball Strategy

Sometimes referred to as Debt Stacking or Debt Snowball Avalanche, this tactic has proved very effective and useful in my personal life. This is prioritizing your debts from highest interest rates to lower interest rates and then focus on paying off the highest interest rate debt first while paying the minimum payments on the other debt.

I recommend this approach but finding the lower dollar amount debt balance and paying that amount off first. This will quickly provide you with some extra capital faster that can be utilized towards debt payments.

Once the first debt is paid, use the same payment dollar amount from the payments and apply to the next debt in line. Read Control Your Debt.

For a limited time, get your copy of the Ultimate Budget Planner which is designed by me to organize your debts in an easy snapshot and then converting it to the budget page.

Balance Transfer

Transferring a balance can be a lifesaver at times. I only recommend this strategy if you are responsible and will not be adding more debt to this account.

When you transfer a high balance credit card amount to a lower

APR or 0% APR for an agreed upon period of time, you are basically saving time on interest payments. If you perform this strategy, you need to really focus on this debt fast before the APR kicks in.

Remember that opening a new account may potentially have a negative impact on your credit score so I would use caution. Sometimes the impact can be a 10-point decline. In some cases, this may be worth it to get out of debt faster but shop around.

Getting a consumer loan to replace credit cards has its perks as well but only if the credit cards are discontinued by your refusing to use. Read more on 3 Top Reasons to Get a Consumer Loan to Payoff Credit Cards.

Earn Extra Income

This is to go without saying but you have to either reduce your expenses and/or increase your income. Having extra money available can be a blessing when in debt because it helps to make the debt payments. Read my blog, 5 Best Part-Time Jobs, on my recommended part-time jobs that have delivered me extra income in the past.

If you have the passion and motivation to no longer be a slave to debt, then listen to King Solomon and let's work towards financial freedom and paying off our lenders.

---

[1] Csiszar, John. Recommended Budget Percentages: How Much Should You Spend? 31 January 2018. Go Banking Rates.

https://www.gobankingrates.com/saving-money/budgeting/recommended-budget-percentages/

[2] Keefe, Jenny. How to Stop Spending. 1 January 2018.

https://www.moneysavingexpert.com/family/stop-spending-budgeting-tool/

STEP 5

Effortless Ways to Build Savings

& Retirement

Almost all of us worry about our financial security and our savings for retirement. We sometimes may imagine what it would be like to not have any savings and have to survive on the pittance that will be available to us through Social Security. We probably imagine living on the streets, on charity, or otherwise dependent on other people just to survive. While those images are a reality for too many people, they do not have to be. Here are three tips to get you started on the road to financial security.

Pay yourself first. Before you pay the first bill or even spend the first dime, set money aside for yourself in a savings vehicle such as a money market or savings account. It is ideal if you can have the savings deducted from your paycheck so you will be even less likely to miss it, but if you cannot, make sure that you pay yourself first. Ideally, you should pay yourself at least ten percent of your gross income, but that is a daunting amount for many people. If you cannot do even five percent, start with just a percent or two. Just two percent on a two thousand dollar monthly salary comes up to $480 a year. While it may take a couple of years, with interest and raises you be putting away $1,000 or $2,000 a year in just a few years.

Live below your means. For some of us, as the saying goes, we have "champagne tastes on a beer budget." We want the best even if we do not need the best. We want the designer sunglasses when a pair of the $10 rack will do just fine. We want the two bedroom apartment next to the pool in the exclusive complex even though we would fit in better in a one bedroom at a safe, but average complex. We want to have our cake and eat it too. That is human nature, but that nature comes with a price. Often that price is living beyond our means and piling up debt. Instead of buying $250 sunglasses, buy a $25 pair and take good care of them. Put the extra into savings or into paying off a debt. Live in the average neighborhood and put the difference toward saving for a house. Live below your means and do not worry about keeping up with everybody else. It may be unrewarding in the short run, but it will be worth it when you do not have to endure the financial pain that your friends do.

Make your money work for you. Since almost every country in the world uses a fiat currency of one type or another, inflation is a very real concern when it comes to saving money. The reason for this is that fiat currencies are not supported by whichever real assets such as silver or gold. Fiat currencies are supported by the government or bank that distributed them. Because of this, the more money that is printed, the less than the individual denomination of currency is worth and the more that people demand of that currency to provide a good or service. In good times inflation may only be between two and three percent, but that means that the value of the money you have saved declines by that amount each year. Unfortunately, the only way to overcome inflation is to make your money work for you. If you let it work in a traditional savings account, you may only make enough to keep pace with inflation. A money market or certificate of deposit will get you a little more, but not a whole lot. The most well-known investment market will provide an average return of about eight percent, but there will be years that you will lose many times more than that. Since all of these investment vehicles carry risk, the key to making your money work for you is to learn when and why your money needs to be placed in any certain vehicle. It will take some work, but learning how to invest your money is vital since it is unlikely that you will simply be able to save enough to provide for your security.

We have looked at three keys for obtaining financial security and retirement savings. There are certainly many more things that you can do from clipping coupons to getting a second job, but virtually none of those items will provide you with the security you will get if you learn these three keys--paying yourself first, living below your means, and making your money work for you.

Do You Count on Social Security for Retirement?

Many people believe that Social Security will not be around after 10 or 15 more years, while others have much faith in the government that they will figure out a way to keep it going. Have you thought about this? What is your opinion on the current situation of the US government and the Social Security program? Do you think relying on Social Security is a solid plan for retirement? Is this your only plan for retirement?

I think that Social Security will be around for a long time. I'm not sure what the government will do about its current fiscal deficit and pay for all of the people retiring. I do have faith that something will be figured out, no matter how old you are today, which you too should be able to receive Social Security benefits. I can only imagine what would happen to some of the politicians who might vote against the S.S.I program. This will probably not go over so well with many Americans.

People who live on S.S, usually only have enough to provide the basics of life. The basics of life include food, clothing, and a roof over your head. Do you want to retire to only having the basics of life because you have relied on Social Security only? Even if Social Security is around when you retire, you should not rely solely on this income to provide for you during your retirement years.

Even if you are 55 years old and had no money in a retirement account, it is not too late to start saving. You can check with your current employer to see if they offer or matched retirement savings. Many times, people that are older than 50 years old with no retirement accounts can use accelerated retirement, which allows them to contribute more to her retirement account tax-free than younger people. There are many different advantages you can take control of right away to start helping your future. Your countenance is one of your best friends and resources to start talking with about your different options. Make sure you maintain your standard of living by planning for the future. After all, if you fail to plan, you're planning to fail.

401k's are the most popular of additional compensation given to employees by companies. Each 401k plan is different for each company. However, all of them allow the employees to make contributions to various assets. These assets can include index funds, mutual funds, stocks, bonds, and even company stock. In most cases, the employers will even match a certain percentage of the contributions made out of each employee's paycheck. However, 401k's offer other advantages as well:

1. The power of compounding and deferred taxes.

The main advantage of 401k's for employees is that you can grow the money in these plans through investing and defer paying taxes on contributions until you withdraw the funds.

2. 401k's are highly portable retirement accounts.

Also, most 401ks are portable allowing you to take them with you once you leave a company. This means you can take the funds and put them in your new company's 401k without too much difficulty.

3. Save money for companies.

Employers like it because it is a way of avoiding having to pay a guaranteed income for pension plans and provides an alternative to employees for compensation purposes in recruitment. Allowing companies to save money here can often create benefits for workers in other ways, such as a business and job itself, higher salaries, etc.

However, 401k's are not without some disadvantages as well. Some of their more common detractors include:

1. Limited investment options.

One of the most common complaints of 401ks is a lack of investing options. This is a particularly contentious one because you have some employees who become overwhelmed with too many choices and want a scaled-down option list and there are others who want to be able to put their funds to work in all kinds of different asset classes.

2. Higher risk than guaranteed pension plans.

Beyond the concern about lack of 401k investment options is that 401k's bring a higher level of risk than guaranteed pension plans. Many employees have seen their 401k's drop significantly in the fall of 2008 showing the riskiness of 401k plans. With reasons like these, there has been a bit of backlash against 401ks although they will likely remain the most popular extra compensation for companies shortly.

With all this said, 401k's can be a very effective tool in helping people save money towards retirement. However, as with any investment option, you need to give it the due diligence it deserves. The recent drop in many workers' 401k plan's values shows that you cannot and should not implement the strategy of putting your money in a 401k and not following it. Instead, the better advice is to periodically monitor your plan and make adjustments on planned spikes in risk. This will help provide you a greater chance to guard yourself against wide swings in the market even if it does require little additional work in monitoring your different investment options.

When planning for retirement, people have lots of options to choose and with so many options, it can be confusing on which is best. In this chapter, I will highlight several of the most popular types of retirement strategies but I highly encourage you to discuss your financial circumstance with a Certified Financial Planner (CFP) because everyone's financial situation and end goal are usually different.

Some family members wish to leave their children their estate while others do not. Some wish to leave an inheritance while other parents do not (true story).

The key to investing is keeping expenses low, having diversification, and hiring a CFP that you can meet with quarterly to discuss any changes within your portfolio. Discuss with the planner about the following to see which is the best option for your circumstance:

-Annuities

-403(b)

-401(k)

-Individual Retirement Accounts

-Corporate Retirement Plans

-Self Employed 401(k)

-Simplified Employee Pension Plan

-Savings Incentive Match Plans for Employees (SIMPLEs)

With so many options available, you can see why it can be difficult to pick. I do highly suggest you max out the annual contribution limits for the 401(K) and IRA if possible.

STEP 6

Achieve Life-Changing Wealth

One of the most important lessons I've learned from banking, investing, and becoming an entrepreneur, is you can only build wealth by having multiple levels of income. This typically scares most people because they immediately think they have to work more hours or get a second job.

To be frank with you, one of the most important lessons to learn from the 2007/2008 Great Recession is to have more than one source of income. How many workers lost their jobs? It didn't matter if you worked construction, worked on Wall Street, sold burgers. With no money being pumped into the economy, people were scared to buy anything. No money being spent means no customers. This let the U.S. unemployment rate to spike up. It took several years to recover from that, and I use "recover" loosely.

For those who studied the wealthy very closely, we learned a few things. The ones who weathered the financial storm the best were those receiving incomes from multiple avenues. In the financial industry, this can be labeled as diversification. It is not only a term used for investing, but for protection as well.

The recession wasn't bad because numerous people lost jobs. It was bad because the American consumer forgot how to save money and manage their finances. Because Joe didn't have 3-6 months of savings, he had to rely on the "broke" U.S. government to bail him out. This came in the form of unemployment.

According to the author of *Rich Habits*, Tom Corley writes "65% of self-made millionaires had three streams of income...29% of self-made millionaires had five or more streams of income".

So what are your options for getting more streams of income? The first is probably obvious but it is what most millionaires have. Most have their own business. This takes time to achieve a regular stream of income but it is a must. It is one reason why I ventured into many online businesses before creating DollarOtter.com.

Other options may include becoming a blogger, or a writer. Writers find great sources of income by selling ebooks through Amazon, writing articles on Medium, and helping reporters with information through HARO.

You can start an online business. I once watched a YouTube video of a couple who shopped at Goodwill stores for luggage and golf bags only to sell these on eBay allowing them to pay off several thousands of dollar of debt.

If investing is one of your fortes, I have an article about investing through alternative investments that pay regular dividends. While you should never use this a single source of income, the dividends and interest payments made to you are regular recurring income.

Note: I recommend you discuss any investment strategies or investing in stocks, equities, fixed income, and alternative investments with a licensed financial advisor prior to taking any action.

Once these incomes are generating an income stream, you find and search for other opportunities to do the same. It never ends because the wealthy have learned, you should always be creating wealth.

The more branches you can grow on your money tree, the less susceptible it is to die from the heat because other branches are protecting the trunk. The trunk is you and your family while the branches are the multiple revenue streams of income.

Conclusion

Achieving financial freedom is a possibility for any household if the patience and persistence are there. By living within your means and having a plan of strategy, you will pay off your debt and reach your retirement goals. Do not become discouraged and do not become distracted by the challenges or obstacles that may present itself.

Be sure to become a subscriber on my finance blog web site at www.dollarotter.com to stay informed and engaged and let's start your financial journey today!